POETRY FROM CRESCENT MOON

William Shakespeare: *Selected Sonnets and Verse*
edited, with an introduction by Mark Tuley

William Shakespeare: *The Sonnets*
edited and introduced by Mark Tuley

*Shakespeare: Love, Poetry and Magic
in Shakespeare's Sonnets and Plays*
by B.D. Barnacle

Edmund Spenser: *Heavenly Love: Selected Poems*
selected and introduced by Teresa Page

Robert Herrick: *Delight In Disorder: Selected Poems*
edited and introduced by M.K. Pace

Sir Thomas Wyatt: *Love For Love: Selected Poems*
selected and introduced by Louise Cooper

John Donne: *Air and Angels: Selected Poems*
selected and introduced by A.H. Ninham

D.H. Lawrence: *Being Alive: Selected Poems*
edited with an introduction by Margaret Elvy

*D.H. Lawrence: Symbolic Landscapes*
by Jane Foster

*D.H. Lawrence: Infinite Sensual Violence*
by M.K. Pace

Percy Bysshe Shelley: *Paradise of Golden Lights: Selected Poems*
selected and introduced by Charlotte Greene

Thomas Hardy: *Her Haunting Ground: Selected Poems*
edited, with an introduction by A.H. Ninham

*Sexing Hardy: Thomas Hardy and Feminism*
by Margaret Elvy

Emily Bronte: *Darkness and Glory: Selected Poems*
selected and introduced by Miriam Chalk

John Keats: *Bright Star: Selected Poems*
edited with an introduction by Miriam Chalk

Henry Vaughan: *A Great Ring of Pure and Endless Light: Selected Poems*
selected and introduced by A.H. Ninham

*The Crescent Moon Book of Love Poetry*
edited by Louise Cooper

*The Crescent Moon Book of Mystical Poetry in English*
edited by Carol Appleby

*The Crescent Moon Book of Nature Poetry From Langland to Lawrence*
edited by Margaret Elvy

*The Crescent Moon Book of Metaphysical Poetry*
edited and introduced by Charlotte Greene

*The Crescent Moon Book of Elizabethan Love Poetry*
edited and introduced by Carol Appleby

*The Crescent Moon Book of Romantic Poetry*
edited and introduced by L.M. Poole

*Blinded By Her Light The Love-Poetry of Robert Graves*
by Jeremy Mark Robinson

*The Best of Peter Redgrove's Poetry: The Book of Wonders*
by Peter Redgrove, edited and introduced by Jeremy Mark Robinson

*Peter Redgrove: Here Comes the Flood*
by Jeremy Mark Robinson

*Sex-Magic-Poetry-Cornwall: A Flood of Poems*
by Peter Redgrove, edited with an essay by Jeremy Mark Robinson

*Brigitte's Blue Heart*
by Jeremy Reed

*Claudia Schiffer's Red Shoes*
by Jeremy Reed

*By-Blows: Uncollected Poems*
by D.J. Enright

*Petrarch, Dante and the Troubadours: The Religion of Love and Poetry*
by Cassidy Hughes

Dante: *Selections From the Vita Nuova*
translated by Thomas Okey

Arthur Rimbaud: *Selected Poems*
edited and translated by Andrew Jary

Arthur Rimbaud: *A Season in Hell*
edited and translated by Andrew Jary

*Rimbaud: Arthur Rimbaud and the Magic of Poetry*
by Jeremy Mark Robinson

Friedrich Hölderlin: *Hölderlin's Songs of Light: Selected Poems*
translated by Michael Hamburger

Rainer Maria Rilke: *Dance the Orange:* Selected Poems
translated by Michael Hamburger

*Rilke: Space, Essence and Angels in the Poetry of Rainer Maria Rilke*
by B.D. Barnacle

*German Romantic Poetry: Goethe, Novalis, Heine, Hölderlin*
by Carol Appleby

Arseny Tarkovsky: *Life, Life: Selected Poems*
translated by Virginia Rounding

Emily Dickinson: *Wild Nights: Selected Poems*
selected and introduced by Miriam Chalk

*Cavafy: Anatomy of a Soul*
by Matt Crispin

# Upon Julia's Breasts:
# Love Poems

# Upon Julia's Breasts

## Love Poems

### Robert Herrick

Edited by M.K. Pace

CRESCENT MOON

CRESCENT MOON PUBLISHING
P.O. Box 1312, Maidstone
Kent, ME14 5XU
Great Britain
www.crmoon.com

First published 2017.
Introduction © M.K. Pace, 1996, 2008, 2017.

Printed and bound in the U.S.A.
Set in Book Antiqua Book 11 on 16pt.
Designed by Radiance Graphics.

The right of M.K. Pace to be identified as the editor of this book has been asserted generally in accordance with sections 77 and 78 of the Copyright, Designs and Patents Act 1988.

All rights reserved. No part of this book may be reprinted or reproduced, stored in a retrieval system, or transmitted, in any form or by any means, electronic, mechanical, photocopying, recording or otherwise, without permission from the publisher.

British Library Cataloguing in Publication data available

*ISBN-13 9781861715876*

*Contents*

A Note On the Text    13

Cherrie-Ripe    17
To Julia    18
Fresh Cream and Cheese    19
To Roses in Julia's Bosom    20
Upon Julia's Breasts    21
Upon the Nipples of Julia's Breast    22
To Julia    23
To Julia    24
On Julia's Breath    25
Her Legs    26
Upon Her Blush    27
Upon Julia's Voice    30
Upon Julia's Lips    29
Upon Her Eyes    30
Upon Her Feet    31
Upon Her Voice    32
Upon Julia's Sweat    33
The Candor of Julia's Teeth    34
Upon Julia's Clothes    35
Cherry-Pit    36
Upon Julia's Unlacing Herself    37
To Daisies, not to shut so soone    38
Delight in Disorder    39
His request to Julia    40
Her Bed    41

The Parliament of Roses to Julia   42
The Weeping Cherry   43
The Lawne   44
The Pomander Bracelet   45
To his Mistresse   46
His sailing from Julia   47
The Rosarie   48
The Rock of Rubies: and The quarrie of Pearls   49
Upon Roses   50
The Frozen Zone: or, Julia disdainfull   51
Teares are Tongues   52
To Julia   53
A Ring presented to Julia   54
Upon Julia's Riband   56
Julia's Petticoat   57
The Captiv'd Bee: or, The Little Filcher   58
The Perfume   60
The silken Snake   61
The Braclet to Julia   62
Upon his Julia   63
On Julia's Picture   64
To Julia in the Temple   65
Upon Julia's haire fill'd with Dew   66
Another on her   67
To Julia, the Flaminica Dialis, or Queen-Priest   68
Art Above Nature; To Julia   69
To Julia   70
The Night-Piece to Julia   71
The Rainbow: or curious Covenant   72
Love palpable   73
Upon the Roses in Julia's bosom   74
The Bride-Cake   75

The Maiden-blush    76
The Transfiguration    77
To Julia, in Her Dawn, or Daybreak    78
Upon Love    79
To Julia    80
The Sacrifice    81
How his soule came ensnared    82
Upon Julia's haire, bundled up in a golden net    83
Upon Julia's washing her self in the river    84
To Julia    85
The Deluge    86
His Covenant or Protestation to Julia    87
The Frozen Heart    88
No Loathsomnesse in love    89
To His Mistress (Objecting to Him
    Neither Toying or Talking)    90
Of Love: A Sonnet    91
Love me little, love me long    92
On himself    93
The cruell Maid    94
His misery in a Mistress    96
A Meditation For His Mistress    97
Upon Love    98
The Kisse. A Dialogue    99
A short hymne to Venus    101
A Hymne to Venus, and Cupid    102
Another upon her    103
Upon the losse of his Mistresses    104
Upon Julia's Recovery    105
Love dislikes nothing    106
Lovers, How They Come and Part    107
Love Lightly Pleased    108
On Love    109

Upon Parting     110
His Mistress To Him At His Farewell     111
His embalming to Julia     112
His last request to Julia     113
To Julia     114
His charge to Julia at his death     115

Illustrations     117
A Note On Robert Herrick     123
Notes     130
Bibliography     131

A NOTE ON THE TEXT

The poems in this edition is taken from the 1885 edition (2nd ed.), edited by Henry Morley, and published by Routledge and Sons, London.

I have modernized some of the spellings in Robert Herrick's poems, but have kept his capitalizations and use of italics. These are part of the flavour of Herrick's verse, and do not detract, I think, from the power or nuance of his poetry.

The poems addressed to Julia come mainly from Herrick's secular book *Hesperides*.

Robert Herrick

Cherrie-Ripe

Cherrie-Ripe, Ripe, Ripe, I cry,
Full and faire ones; come and buy:
If so be, you ask me where
They doe grow? I answer, There,
Where my Julia's lips doe smile;
There's the Land, or Cherry-Ile:
Whose Plantations fully show
All the yeere, where Cherries grow.

To Julia

How rich and pleasing thou my *Julia* art
In each thy dainty, and peculiar part!
First, thy *Queen-ship* on thy head is set
Of flowers a sweet commingled Coronet:
About thy neck a Carkanet is bound,
Made of the *Rubie, Pearle* and *Diamond*:
A golden ring, that shines upon thy thumb:
About thy wrist, the rich *Dardanium*.
Between thy Breasts (than Down of Swans more white)
There plays the *Sapphire* with the *Chrysolite*.
No part besides must of thy selfe be known,
But by the *Topaz, Opal, Calcedon*.

Fresh Cheese and Cream

Wo'd yee have fresh Cheese and Cream?
Julia's Breast can give you them:
And if more; Each Nipple cries,
To your Cream, her's Strawberries.

To Roses in Julia's Bosom


Roses, you can never die,
Since the place wherein ye lye,
Heat and moisture mixt are so,
As to make ye ever grow.

Upon Julia's breasts

Display thy breasts, my Julia, there let me
Behold that circummortall purity:
Betweene whose glories, there my lips I'll lay,
Ravisht, in that faire Via Lactea.

Upon the Nipples of Julia's Breast

Have ye beheld (with much delight)
A red-Rose peeping through a white?
Or else a Cherrie (double grac't)
Within a Lillie? Center plac't?
Or ever mark't the pretty beam,
A Strawberry shewes halfe drown'd in Creame?
Or seen rich Rubies blushing through
A pure smooth Pearle, and Orient too?
So like to this, nay all the rest,
Is each neate Niplet of her breast.

To Julia

Holy waters hither bring
For the sacred sprinkling:
Baptize me and thee, and so
Let us to the Altar go.
And (ere we our rites commence)
Wash our hands in innocence.
Then I'll be the Rex Sacrorum,
Thou the Queen of Peace and Quorum.

To Julia

Help me, Julia, for to pray,
Mattens sing, or Mattens say:
This I know, the Fiend will fly
Far away, if thou beest by.
Bring the Holy-water hither;
Let us wash, and pray together:
When our Beads are thus united,
Then the Foe will fly affrighted.

On Julia's breath

Breathe, Julia, breathe, and I'll protest,
Nay more, I'll deeply sweare,
That all the Spices of the East
Are circumfused there.

Her Legs

Fain would I kiss my Julia's dainty Leg,
Which is as white and hair-less as an egge.

Upon her blush

When Julia blushes, she do's show
Cheeks like to Roses, when they blow.

Upon Julia's Voice

So smooth, so sweet, so silv'ry is thy voice,
As, could they hear, the Damn'd would make no noise,
But listen to thee, (walking in thy chamber)
Melting melodious words, to Lutes of Amber.

On Julia's lips

Sweet are my Julia's lips and cleane,
As if or'e washt in Hippocrene.

Upon her Eyes

Cleere are her eyes,
Like purest Skies.
Discovering from thence
A Babie there
That turns each Sphere,
Like an Intelligence.

Upon her feet

Her pretty feet
Like snailes did creep
A little out, and then,
As if they started at Bo-peep,
Did soon draw in agen.

Upon her Voice

Let but thy voice engender with the string,
And Angels will be borne, while thou dost sing.

Upon Julia's sweat

Wo'd ye oyle of Blossomes get?
Take it from my Julia's sweat:
Oyl of Lillies, and of Spike,
From her moysture take the like:
Let her breath, or let her blow,
All rich spices thence will flow.

The Candor of Julia's teeth

White as Zenobias teeth, the which the Girles
Of Rome did weare for their most precious Pearles.

Upon Julia's Clothes

When as in silks my Julia goes, (flowes
Then, then (me thinks) how sweetly
That liquefaction of her clothes.

Next, when I cast mine eyes and see
That brave Vibration each way free;
O how that glittering taketh me!

Cherry-pit

Julia and I did lately sit
Playing for sport, at Cherry-pit:
She threw; I cast; and having thrown,
I got the Pit, and she the Stone.

Upon Julia's Unlacing Herself


Tell, if thou canst, (and truly) whence doth come
This *Camphire, Storax, Spiknard, Galbanum*:
These *Musks,* these *Ambers,* and those other smells
(Sweet as the *vestrie of the Oracles*.)
I'll tell thee; while my *Julia* did unlace
Her silken bodies, but a breathing space:
The passive Aire such odour then assum'd,
As when to *Jove* Great *Juno* goes perfum'd.
Whose pure-Immortal body doth transmit
A scent, that fills both Heaven and Earth with it.

To Daisies, not to shut so soone

Shut not so soon; the dull-ey'd night
Ha's not as yet begunne
To make a seisure on the light,
Or to seale up the Sun.

No Marigolds yet closed are;
No shadowes great appeare;
Nor doth the early Shepheards Starre
Shine like a spangle here.

Stay but till my Julia close
Her life-begetting eye;
And let the whole world then dispose
It selfe to live or dye.

Delight in Disorder


A sweet disorder in the dresse
Kindles in cloathes a wantonnesse:
A Lawne about the shoulders thrown
Into a fine distraction:
An erring Lace, which here and there
Enthralls the Crimson Stomacher:
A Cuffe neglectfull, and thereby
Ribbands to flow confusedly:
A winning wave (deserving Note)
In the tempestuous petticote:
A carelesse shooe-string, in whose tye
I see a wilde civility:
Doe more bewitch me, then when Art
Is too precise in every part.

His request to Julia


Julia, if I chance to die
Ere I print my Poetry;
I most humbly thee desire
To commit it to the fire:
Better 'twere my Book were dead,
Then to live not perfected.

Her Bed

See'st, thou that Cloud as silver cleare,
Plump, soft, & swelling every where?
Tis Julia's Bed, and she sleeps there.

The Parliament of Roses to Julia

I dreamt the Roses one time went
To meet and sit in Parliament:
The place for these, and for the rest
Of flowers, was thy spotlesse breast:
Over the which a State was drawne
Of Tiffanie, or Cob-web Lawne;
Then in that Parly, all those powers
Voted the Rose; the Queen of flowers.
But so, as that her self should be
The maide of Honour unto thee.

The Weeping Cherry

I saw a Cherry weep, and why?
Why wept it? but for shame,
Because my Julia's lip was by,
And did out-red the same.
But pretty Fondling, let not fall
A teare at all for that:
Which Rubies, Corralls, Scarlets, all
For tincture, wonder at.

The Lawne

Wo'd I see Lawn, clear as the Heaven, and thin?
It sho'd be onely in my Julia's skin:
Which so betrayes her blood, as we discover
The blush of cherries, when a Lawn's cast over.

The Pomander Bracelet

To me my Julia lately sent
A Bracelet richly Redolent:
The Beads I kist, but most lov'd her
That did perfume the Pomander.

To his Mistresse


Choose me your Valentine;
Next, let us marry:
Love to the death will pine,
If we long tarry.

Promise, and keep your vowes,
Or vow ye never:
Loves doctrine disallowes
Troth-breakers ever.

You have broke promise twice
(Deare) to undoe me;
If you prove faithlesse thrice,
None then will wooe you.

His sailing from Julia


When that day comes, whose evening sayes I'm gone
Unto that watrie Desolation:
Devoutly to thy Closet-gods then pray,
That my wing'd ship may meet no Remora.
Those Deities which circum-walk the Seas,
And look upon our dreadfull passages,
Will from all dangers, re-deliver me,
For one drink-offering, poured out by thee.
Mercie and Truth live with thee! and forbeare
(In my short absence) to unsluce a teare:
But yet for Loves-sake, let thy lips doe this,
Give my dead picture one engendring kisse:
Work that to life, and let me ever dwell
In thy remembrance (Julia.) So farewell.

The Rosarie

One ask'd me where the Roses grew?
I bade him not goe seek;
But forthwith bade my Julia shew
A bud in either cheek.

The Rock of Rubies: and The quarrie of Pearls

Some ask'd me where the Rubies grew?
And nothing I did say:
But with my finger pointed to
The lips of Julia.
Some ask'd how Pearls did grow, and where?
Then spoke I to my Girle,
To part her lips, and shew'd them there
The Quarelets of Pearl.

Upon Roses

Under a Lawne, then skyes more cleare,
Some ruffled Roses nestling were:
And snugging there, they seem'd to lye
As in a flowrie Nunnery:
They blush'd, and look'd more fresh then flowers
Quickned of late by Pearly showers;
And all, because they were possest
But of the heat of Julia's breast:
Which as a warme, and moistned spring,
Gave them their ever flourishing.

The Frozen Zone:
or, Julia disdainfull


Whither? Say, whither shall I fly,
To slack these flames wherein I frie?
To the Treasures, shall I goe,
Of the Raine, Frost, Haile, and Snow?
Shall I search the under-ground,
Where all Damps, and Mists are found?
Shall I seek (for speedy ease)
All the floods, and frozen seas?
Or descend into the deep,
Where eternall cold does keep?
These may coole; but there's a Zone
Colder yet then any one:
That's my Julia's breast; where dwels
Such destructive Ysicles;
As that the Congelation will
Me sooner starve, then those can kill.

Teares are Tongues


When Julia chid, I stood as mute the while,
As is the fish, or tonguelesse Crocadile.
Aire coyn'd to words, my Julia co'd not heare;
But she co'd see each eye to stamp a teare:
By which, mine angry Mistresse might descry,
Teares are the noble language of the eye.
And when true love of words is destitute,
The Eyes by tears speak, while the Tongue is mute.

To Julia


Permit me, Julia, now to goe away;
Or by thy love, decree me here to stay.
If thou wilt say, that I shall live with thee;
Here shall my endless Tabernacle be:
If not, (as banisht) I will live alone
There, where no language ever yet was known.

A Ring presented to Julia

Julia, I bring
To thee this Ring.
Made for thy finger fit;
To shew by this,
That our love is
(Or sho'd be) like to it.

Close though it be,
The joynt is free:
So when Love's yoke is on,
It must not gall,
Or fret at all
With hard oppression.

But it must play
Still either way;
And be, too, such a yoke,
As not too wide,
To over-slide;
Or be so strait to choak.

So we, who beare,
This beame, must reare
Our selves to such a height:
As that the stay
Of either may
Create the burden light.

And as this round
Is no where found
To flaw, or else to sever:
So let our love
As endless prove;
And pure as Gold for ever.

Upon Julia's Riband

As shews the Aire, when with a Rain-bow grac'd;
So smiles that Riband 'bout my Julia's waste:
Or like---Nay 'tis that Zonulet of love,
Wherein all pleasures of the world are wove.

Julia's Petticoat

Thy Azure Robe I did behold,
As airy as the leaves of gold,
Which, erring here, and wand'ring there,
Pleas'd with transgression everywhere:
Sometimes 'twould pant, and sigh, and heave,
As if to stir it scarce had leave:
But having got it; thereupon
'Twould make a brave expansion.
And pound'd with stars it show'd to me
Like a *Celestiall Canopie*.
Sometimes 'twould blaze, and then abate,
Like to a flame grown moderate:
Sometimes away 'twould wildly fling,
Then to thy thighs so closely cling
That some conceit did melt me down,
As lovers fall into a swoon:
And, all confus'd, I there did lie
Drown'd in Delights, but could not die.
That Leading Cloud I follow'd still,
Hoping t'have seen of it my fill;
But ah! I could not: should it move
To Life Eternal, I could love.

The Captiv'd Bee:
or, The Little Filcher


As Julia once a-slumb'ring lay,
It chanc't a Bee did flie that way,
(After a dew, or dew-like shower)
To tipple freely in a flower.
For some rich flower, he took the lip
Of Julia, and began to sip;
But when he felt he suckt from thence
Hony, and in the quintessence:
He drank so much he scarce co'd stir;
So Julia took the Pilferer.
And thus surpriz'd (as Filchers use)
He thus began himselfe t'excuse:
Sweet Lady-Flower, I never brought
Hither the least one theeving thought:
But taking those rare lips of yours
For some fresh, fragrant, luscious flowers:
I thought I might there take a taste,
Where so much sirrop ran at waste.
Besides, know this, I never sting
The flower that gives me nourishing:
But with a kisse, or thanks, doe pay
For Honie, that I beare away.
This said, he laid his little scrip
Of hony, 'fore her Ladiship:
And told her, (as some tears did fall)
That, that he took, and that was all.

At which she smil'd; and bade him goe
And take his bag; but thus much know,
When next he came a pilfring so,
He sho'd from her full lips derive,
Hony enough to fill his hive.

The Perfume

To-morrow, Julia, I betimes must rise,
For some small fault, to offer sacrifice:
The Altar's ready; Fire to consume
The fat; breathe thou, and there's the rich perfume.

The silken Snake

For sport my Julia threw a Lace
Of silke and silver at my face:
Watchet the silke was; and did make
A shew, as if 't 'ad been a snake:
The suddenness did me affright;
But though it scar'd, it did not bite.

The Braclet to Julia

Why I tye about thy wrist,
Julia, this my silken twist;
For what other reason is't,
But to shew thee how in part,
Thou my pretty Captive art?
But thy Bondslave is my heart:
'Tis but silke that bindeth thee,
Knap the thread, and thou art free:
But 'tis otherwise with me;
I am bound, and fast bound so,
That from thee I cannot go;
If I co'd, I wo'd not so.

## Upon his Julia

Will ye heare, what I can say
Briefly of my Julia?
Black and rowling is her eye,
Double chinn'd, and forehead high:
Lips she has, all Rubie red,
Cheeks like Creame Enclarited:
And a nose that is the grace
And Proscenium of her face.
So that we may guesse by these,
The other parts will richly please.

On Julia's Picture

How am I ravisht! When I do but see,
The Painters art in thy Sciography?
If so, how much more shall I dote thereon,
When once he gives it incarnation?

To Julia in the Temple


Besides us two, i'th' Temple here's not one
To make up now a Congregation.
Let's to the Altar of perfumes then go,
And say short Prayers; and when we have done so,
Then we shall see, how in a little space,
Saints will come in to fill each Pew and Place.

Upon Julia's haire fill'd with Dew

Dew sate on Julia's haire,
And spangled too,
Like Leaves that laden are
With trembling Dew:
Or glitter'd to my sight,
As when the Beames
Have their reflected light,
Daunc't by the Streames.

Another on her

How can I choose but love, and follow her,
Whose shadow smels like milder Pomander!
How can I chuse but kisse her, whence do's come
The Storax, Spiknard, Myrrhe, and Ladanum.

To Julia, the Flaminica Dialis,
or Queen-Priest


Thou know'st, my Julia, that it is thy turne
This Mornings Incense to prepare, and burne.
The Chaplet, and * Inarculum here be,
With the white Vestures, all attending Thee.
This day, the Queen-Priest, thou art made t'appease
Love for our very-many Trespasses.
One chiefe transgression is among the rest,
Because with Flowers her Temple was not drest:
The next, because her Altars did not shine
With daily Fyers: The last, neglect of Wine:
For which, her wrath is gone forth to consume
Us all, unlesse preserv'd by thy Perfume.
Take then thy Censer; Put in Fire, and thus,
O Pious-Priestresse! make a Peace for us.
For our neglect, Love did our Death decree,
That we escape. Redemption comes by Thee.

Art above Nature, to Julia


When I behold a Forrest spread
With silken trees upon thyhead;
And when I see that other Dresse
Of flowers set in comlinesse:
When I behold another grace
In the ascent of curious Lace,
Which like a Pinacle doth shew
The top, and the top-gallant too.
Then, when I see thy Tresses bound
Into an Ovall, square, or round;
And knit in knots far more then I
Can tell by tongue; or true-love tie:
Next, when those Lawnie Filmes I see
Play with a wild civility:
And all those airie silks to flow,
Alluring me, and tempting so:
I must confesse, mine eye and heart
Dotes less on Nature, then on Art.

To Julia


The Saints-bell calls; and, Julia, I must read
The Proper Lessons for the Saints now dead:
To grace which Service, Julia, there shall be
One Holy Collect, said or sung for Thee.
Dead when thou art, Deare Julia, thou shalt have
A Tentrall sung by Virgins o're thy Grave:
Meane time we two will sing the Dirge of these;
Who dead, deserve our best remembrances.

The Night-Piece to Julia

Her Eyes the Glow-worm lend thee,
The Shooting Starres attend thee;
      And the Elves also,
      Whose little eyes glow
Like the sparks of fire, befriend thee.

No *Will-o'-the-Wispe* mislight thee,
Nor Snake or Slow-worm bite thee;
      But on, on thy way
      Not making a stay,
Since Ghost there's none to affright thee.

Let not the dark thee cumber:
What though the Moon does slumber?
      The Starres of the night
      Will lend thee their light
Like Tapers clear without number.

Then *Julia*, let me woo thee,
Thus, thus to come unto me;
      And when I shall meet
      Thy silv'ry feet
My soul I'll pour into thee.

The Rainbow: or curious Covenant

Mine eyes, like clouds, were drizling raine,
And as they thus did entertaine
The gentle Beams from Julia's sight
To mine eyes level'd opposite:
O Thing admir'd! there did appeare
A curious Rainbow smiling there;
Which was the Covenant, that she
No more wo'd drown mine eyes, or me.

Love palpable

I prest my Julia's lips, and in the kisse
Her Soule and Love were palpable in this.

Upon the Roses in Julia's bosom


Thrice happie Roses, so much grac't, to have
Within the Bosome of my Love your grave.
Die when ye will, your sepulchre is knowne,
Your Grave her Bosome is, the Lawne the Stone.

The Bride-Cake

This day my Julia thou must make
For Mistresse Bride, the wedding Cake:
Knead but the Dow and it will be
To paste of Almonds turn'd by thee:
Or kisse it thou, but once, or twice,
And for the Bride-Cake ther'l be Spice.

The Maiden-blush

So look the mornings when the Sun
Paints them with fresh Vermilion:
So Cherries blush, and Kathern Peares,
And Apricocks, in youthfull yeares:
So Corrolls looke more lovely Red,
And Rubies lately polished:
So purest Diaper doth shine,
Stain'd by the Beames of Clarret wine:
As Julia looks when she doth dress
Her either cheeke with bashfullness.

The Transfiguration

Immortall clothing I put on,
So soone as Julia I am gon
To mine eternall Mansion.

Thou, thou art here, to humane sight
Cloth'd all with incorrupted light;
But yet how more admir'dly bright

Wilt thou appear, when thou art set
In thy refulgent Thronelet,
That shin'st thus in thy counterfeit?

To Julia, in Her Dawn, or Daybreak

By the next kindling of the day
   My *Julia* thou shalt see,
Ere *Ave-Mary* thou canst say
   I'll come and visit thee.

Yet ere thou counsl'st with thy Glasse,
   Appeare thou to mine eyes
As smooth, and nak't, as she that was
   The prime of *Paradise*.

If blush thou must, then blush thou through
   A Lawn, that thou mayst looke
As purest Pearles, or Pebbles do
   When peeping through a Brooke.

As Lilies shrin'd in Christall, so
   Do thou to me appeare;
Or Damask Roses, when they grow
   To sweet acquaintance there.

Upon Love

Some salve to every sore, we may apply;
Only for my wound there's no remedy.
Yet if my Julia kisse me, there will be
A soveraign balme found out to cure me.

To Julia

I am zeallesse, prethee pray
For my well-fare (Julia)
For I thinke the gods require
Male perfumes, but Female fire.

The Sacrifice, by way of Discourse betwixt
himselfe and Julia

*Herr.* Come and let's in solemn wise
Both addresse to sacrifice:
Old Religion first commands
That we wash our hearts, and hands.
Is the beast exempt from staine,
Altar cleane, no fire prophane?
Are the Garlands, Is the Nard
*Jul.* Ready here? All well prepar'd,
With the Wine that must be shed
(Twixt the hornes) upon the head
Of the holy Beast we bring
(For our Trespasse-offering.
*Herr.* All is well; now next to these
Put we on pure Surplices;
And with Chaplets crown'd, we'l rost
With perfumes the Holocaust:
And (while we the gods invoke)
Reade acceptance by the smoake.

How his soule came ensnared

My soule would one day goe and seeke
For Roses, and in Julia's cheeke,
A richess of those sweets she found,
(As in an other Rosamond.)
But gathering Roses as she was;
(Not knowing what would come to passe)
It chanst a ringlet of her haire,
Caught my poore soule, as in a snare:
Which ever since has been in thrall,
Yet freedome, shee enjoyes withall.

Upon Julia's haire, bundled up in a golden net

Tell me, what needs those rich deceits,
These golden Toyles, and Trammel-nets,
To take thine haires when they are knowne
Already tame, and all thine owne?
'Tis I am wild, and more then haires
Deserve these Mashes and those snares.
Set free thy Tresses, let them flow
As aires doe breathe, or winds doe blow:
And let such curious Net-works be
Lesse set for them, then spred for me.

Upon Julia's washing her self in the river

How fierce was I, when I did see
My Julia wash her self in thee!
So Lillies thorough Christall look:
So purest pebbles in the brook:
As in the River Julia did,
Halfe with a Lawne of water hid,
Into thy streames my self I threw,
And strugling there, I kist thee too;
And more had done (it is confest)
Had not thy waves forbad the rest.

To Julia


Offer thy gift; but first the Law commands
Thee Julia, first, to sanctifie thy hands:
Doe that my Julia which the rites require,
Then boldly give thine incense to the fire.

The deluge

Drowning, drowning, I espie
Coming from my Julia's eye:
'Tis some solace in our smart,
To have friends to beare a part:
I have none; but must be sure
Th'inundation to endure.
Shall not times hereafter tell
This for no meane miracle;
When the waters by their fall
Threatn'd ruine unto all?
Yet the deluge here was known,
Of a world to drowne but One.

## His Covenant or Protestation to Julia

Why do'st thou wound, & break my heart?
As if we sho'd for ever part?
Hast thou not heard an Oath from me,
After a day, or two, or three,
I wo'd come back and live with thee?
Take, if thou do'st distrust, that Vowe;
This second Protestation now.
Upon thy cheeke that spangel'd Teare,
Which sits as Dew of Roses there:
That Teare shall scarce be dri'd before
I'll kisse the Threshold of thy dore.
Then weepe not sweet; but thus much know,
I'm halfe return'd before I go.

The Frozen Heart

I freeze, I freeze, and nothing dwels
In me but Snow, and ysicles.
For pitties sake give your advice,
To melt this snow, and thaw this ice;
I'll drink down Flames, but if so be
Nothing but love can supple me;
I'll rather keepe this frost, and snow,
Then to be thaw'd, or heated so.

No Loathsomnesse in love

What I fancy, I approve,
No Dislike there is in love:
Be my Mistresse short or tall,
And distorted there-withall:
Be she likewise one of those,
That an Acre hath of Nose:
Be her forehead, and her eyes
Full of incongruities:
Be her cheeks so shallow too,
As to shew her Tongue wag through:
Be her lips ill hung, or set,
And her grinders black as jet;
Ha's she thinne haire, hath she none,
She's to me a Paragon.

To His Mistress (Objecting to Him Neither Toying or Talking)

You say I love not, 'cause I do not play
Still with your curls, and kiss the time away.
You blame me too, because I can't devise
Some sport, to please those Babies in your eyes:
By *Love's Religion*, I must here confess it,
The most I love, when I the least express it.
*Small griefs find tongues*: Full Casks are ever found
To give (if any, yet) but little sound.
*Deep waters noiseless are*; and this we know,
*That chiding streams betray small depth below.*
So when Love speechless is, she doth expresse
A depth in love, and that depth, bottomlesse.
Now since my love is tongueless, know me such,
Who speak but little, 'cause I love so much.

Of Love. A Sonnet


How Love came in, I do not know,
Whether by th'eye, or eare, or no:
Or whether with the soule it came
(At first) infused with the same:
Whether in part 'tis here or there,
Or, like the soule, whole every where:
This troubles me: but I as well
As any other, this can tell;
That when from hence she does depart,
The out-let then is from the heart.

Love me little, love me long

You say, to me-wards your affection's strong;
Pray love me little, so you love me long.
Slowly goes farre: The meane is best: Desire
Grown violent, do's either die, or tire.

On himself

Love-sick I am, and must endure
A desp'rate grief, that finds no cure.
Ah me! I try; and trying, prove,
No Herbs have power to cure Love.
Only one Soveraign salve, I know,
And that is Death, the end of Woe.

The cruell Maid


And cruell Maid, because I see
You scornfull of my love, and me:
I'll trouble you no more; but goe
My way, where you shall never know
What is become of me: there I
Will find me out a path to die;
Or learne some way how to forget
You, and your name, for ever: yet
Ere I go hence; know this from me,
What will, in time, your Fortune be:
This to your coynesse I will tell;
And having spoke it once, Farewell.
The Lillie will not long endure;
Nor the Snow continue pure:
The Rose, the Violet, one day
See, both these Lady-flowers decay:
And you must fade, as well as they.
And it may chance that Love may turn,
And (like to mine) make your heart burn
And weep to see't; yet this thing doe,
That my last Vow commends to you:
When you shall see that I am dead,
For pitty let a teare be shed;
And (with your Mantle o're me cast)
Give my cold lips a kisse at last:
If twice you kisse, you need not feare,
That I shall stir, or live more here.

Next, hollow out a Tombe to cover
Me; me, the most despised Lover:
And write thereon, This, Reader, know,
Love kill'd this man. No more but so.

His misery in a Mistress

Water, Water I espie:
Come, and coole ye; all who frie
In your loves; but none as I.

Though a thousand showres be
Still a falling, yet I see
Not one drop to light on me.

Happy you, who can have seas
For to quench ye, or some ease
From your kinder Mistresses.

I have one, and she alone,
Of a thousand thousand known,
Dead to all compassion.

Such an one, as will repeat
Both the cause, and make the heat
More by Provocation great.

Gentle friends, though I despaire
Of my cure, doe you beware
Of those Girles, which cruell are.

A Meditation For His Mistress

You are a *Tulip* seen today,
But (Dearest) of so short a stay
That where you grew scarce man can say.

You are a lovely *July-flower*
Yet one rude wind or ruffling shower
Will force you hence, (and in an hour.)

You are a sparkling *Rose* in' th'bud,
Yet lost ere that chaste flesh and blood
Can show where you or grew or stood.

You are a full-spread, fair-set Vine,
And can with Tendrils love entwine,
Yet dry'd, ere you distil your Wine.

You are like Balme enclosed (well)
In *Amber,* or some *Crystal* shell,
Yet lost ere you transfuse your smell.

You are a dainty *Violet,*
Yet whither'd ere you can be set
Within a Virgin's Coronet.

You are the *Queen* all flowers among,
But die you must (fair Maid) ere long,
As He, the maker of this song.

Upon Love

Love's a thing, (as I do heare)
Ever full of pensive feare;
Rather then to which I'll fall,
Trust me, I'll not like at all:
If to love I should entend,
Let my haire then stand an end:
And that terrour likewise prove,
Fatall to me in my love.
But if horrour cannot slake
Flames, which wo'd an entrance make;
Then the next thing I desire,
Is to love, and live i'th fire.

The Kisse. A Dialogue

Among thy Fancies, tell me this,
What is the thing we call a kisse?
I shall resolve ye, what it is.

It is a creature born and bred
Between the lips, (all cherrie-red,)
By love and warme desires fed,
Chor. And makes more soft the Bridall Bed.

It is an active flame, that flies,
First, to the Babies of the eyes;
And charmes them there with lullabies;
Chor. And stils the Bride too, when she cries.

Then to the chin, the cheek, the eare,
It frisks, and flyes, now here, now there,
'Tis now farre off, and then tis nere;
Chor. And here, and there, and every where.

Ha's it a speaking virtue? Yes;
How speaks it, say? Do you but this,
Part your joyn'd lips, then speaks your kisse;
Chor. And this loves sweetest language is.

Has it a body? I, and wings
With thousand rare encolourings:
And as it flyes, it gently sings,
Chor. Love, honie yeelds; but never stings.

A short hymne to Venus

Goddesse, I do love a Girle
Rubie-lipt, and tooth'd with Pearl:
If so be, I may but prove
Luckie in this Maide I love:
I will promise there shall be
Mirtles offer'd up to Thee.

A Hymne to Venus, and Cupid

Sea-born Goddesse, let me be,
By thy sonne thus grac't, and thee;
That when ere I wooe, I find
Virgins coy, but not unkind.
Let me when I kisse a maid,
Taste her lips, so over-laid
With Loves-sirrop; that I may,
In your Temple, when I pray,
Kisse the Altar, and confess
Ther's in love, no bitterness.

Another upon her


First, for your shape, the curious cannot shew
Any one part that's dissonant in you:
And 'gainst your chast behaviour there's no Plea,
Since you are knowne to be Penelope.
Thus faire and cleane you are, although there be
A mighty strife 'twixt Forme and Chastitie.

Upon the losse of his Mistresses

I have lost, and lately, these
Many dainty Mistresses:
Stately Julia, prime of all;
Sappho next, a principall:
Smooth Anthea, for a skin
White, and Heaven-like Chrystalline:
Sweet Electra, and the choice
Myrha, for the Lute, and Voice.
Next, Corinna, for her wit,
And for the graceful use of it:
With Perilla: All are gone;
Onely Herrick's left alone,
For to number sorrow by
Their depart

Upon Julia's Recovery

Droop, droop no more, or hang the head
Ye Roses almost withered;
Now strength, and newer Purple get,
Each here declining Violet.
O Primroses! let this day be
A Resurrection unto ye;
And to all flowers ally'd in blood,
Or sworn to that sweet Sister-hood:
For Health on Julia's cheek hath shed
Clarret, and Creame commingled.
And those her lips doe now appeare
As beames of Corrall, but more cleare.

Love dislikes nothing

Whatsoever thing I see,
Rich or poore although it be;
'Tis a Mistresse unto mee.

Be my Girle, or faire or browne,
Do's she smile, or do's she frowne:
Still I write a Sweet-heart downe.

Be she rough, or smooth of skin;
When I touch, I then begin
For to let Affection in.

Be she bald, or do's she weare
Locks incurl'd of other haire;
I shall find enchantment there.

Be she whole, or be she rent,
So my fancie be content,
She's to me most excellent.

Be she fat, or be she leane,
Be she sluttish, be she cleane,
I'm a man for ev'ry Sceane.

Lovers, How They Come and Part

A *Gyges'* Ring they bear about them still,
To be, and not seen when and where they will.
They tread on clouds, and though they sometimes fall,
They fall like dew, but make no noise at all.
So silently they one to th'other come,
As colours steal into the Pear or Plum,
And Air-like, leave no pression to be seen
Where e'er they met, or parting place has been.

Love Lightly Pleased

Let fair or foul my mistress be,
Or low, or tall, she pleaseth me;
Or let her walk, or stand, or sit,
The posture her's, I'm pleased with it;
Or let her tongue be still, or stir
Graceful is every thing from her;
Or let her grant, or else deny,
My love will fit each history.

On Love

Love's of itself too sweet; the best of all
Is, when love's honey has a dash of gall.

Upon Parting


Go hence away, and in thy parting know
Tis not my voice, but heavens, that bids thee go;
Spring hence thy faith, nor thinke it ill desert
I find in thee, that makes me thus to part,
But voice of fame, and voice of heaven have
                              thunder'd
We both were, if both of us not sunder'd;
Fold now thine arms, and in thy last look reare
One Sigh of love, and coole it with a teare;
Since part we must Let's kisse, that done retire
With as cold frost, as erst we met with fire;
With such white vows as fate can ne'er dissever
But truth knit fast; and so farewell for ever.

His Mistress To Him At His Farewell

You may vow I'll not forget
To pay the debt
Which to thy memory stands as due
As faith can seal it you.
– Take then tribute of my tears;
So long as I have fears
To prompt me, I shall ever
Languish and look, but thy return see never.
Oh then to lessen my despair,
Print thy lips into(the air,
So by this
Means, I may kiss thy kiss,
Whenas some kind
Wind
Shall hither waft it: – And, in lieu,
My lips shall send a thousand back to you.

His embalming to Julia


For my embalming, Julia, do but this,
Give thou my lips but their supreamest kiss:
Or else trans-fuse thy breath into the chest,
Where my small reliques must for ever rest:
That breath the Balm, the myrrh, the Nard shal be,
To give an incorruption unto me.

His last request to Julia

I have been wanton, and too bold I feare,
To chafe o're much the Virgins cheek or eare:
Beg for my Pardon Julia; He doth winne
Grace with the Gods, who's sorry for his sinne.
That done, my Julia, dearest Julia, come,
And go with me to chuse my Buriall roome:
My Fates are ended; when thy Herrick dyes,
Claspe thou his Book, then close thou up his Eyes.

To Julia


Julia, when thy Herrick dies,
Close thou up thy Poets eyes:
And his last breath, let it be
Taken in by none but Thee.

His charge to Julia at his death


Dearest of thousands, now the time drawes neere,
That with my Lines, my Life must full-stop here.
Cut off thy haires; and let thy Teares be shed
Over my Turfe, when I am buried.
Then for effusions, let none wanting be,
Or other Rites that doe belong to me;
As Love shall helpe thee, when thou do'st go hence
Unto thy everlasting residence.

Title pages of Hesperides by Robert Herrick
(this page and over)

# *HESPERIDES:* OR, THE WORKS BOTH HUMANE & DIVINE OF ROBERT HERRICK *Esq.*

OVID.

*Effugient avidos Carmina nostra Rogos.*

*LONDON,*
Printed for *John Williams,* and *Francis Eglesfield,*
and are to be sold by *Tho: Hunt,* Book-seller
in *Exon.* 1648.

John William Waterhouse, Gather Ye Rosebuds While Ye May, 1909, private collection

John William Waterhouse, Gather Ye Rosebuds While Ye May, 1909

John William Waterhouse, Ophelia (Gather Ye Rosebuds While Ye May), 1909

Elizabeth Stanhope Forbes, A Sweet Disorder In the Dress, 1897-98

# A Note On Robert Herrick

ROBERT HERRICK (1591-1674) was one of the Cavalier poets (other Cavalier poets included Suckling, Carew and Lovelace). He was born in London and lived much of his life in the rough remoteness of a parish in Devonshire. He studied at Cambridge (St John's College and Trinity Hall), graduating in 1617 as a Bachelor of Arts and a Master of Arts in 1620. His law studies were dropped in 1623, and he was ordained as a deacon and priest in 1624. His major work (*Hesperides or The Works both Humane and Divine* of Robert Herrick, Esq.) was published in 1648. There are some 1130 poems in the first, secular part, *Hesperides*, and 272 in *Noble Numbers*, the religious works. F.R. Leavis reckoned that Herrick was 'trivially charming',[1] a view easily refuted by any close perusal of his verse. For T.S. Eliot, Herrick was the paradigmatic 'minor poet'.[2] One can understand how it is that Herrick was for so long viewed in this way. The more one considers his *Hesperides*, though, which one recent critic called 'a seductively sweet, strangely tumultuous exploration of love, art, friendship, festivity, and loss',[3] the greater Robert Herrick becomes.

One of the delights included in this book is Robert Herrick's magnificent 'The Argument of His Book'. This is a truly majestic fourteen-line poem, an invocation to nature, and of humans interacting with nature. It is, essentially, a list-poem, where the poet catalogues the things he will sing about in the rest of his book:

> I sing of *Brooks*, of *Blossomes*, *Birds*, and *Bowers*:
> Of *April*, *May*, of *June*, and *July*-Flowers.
> I sing of *May-poles*, *Hock-carts*, *Wassails*, *Wakes*,
> Of *Bride-grooms*, *Brides*, and of their *Bridall-cakes*.
> I write of *Youth*, of *Love*, and have Accesse
> By these, to sing of cleanly-*Wantonesse*.

Robert Herrick couches his list in simple, dramatic English, a form of direct, powerful English that people since Herrick's time have associated with the (King James) *Bible*. The rest of his poetry (in his *Hesperides*) followed the plan outlined the poem 'The Argument of His Book'. Herrick was particularly well situated, geographically, to write nature poetry. Like Coleridge, Wordsworth and Brontë, Herrick lived in the midst of the countryside – in the relative isolation of Dean Prior, on the edge of Dartmoor in Devon (he compared his exile with that of Ovid and Horace). Herrick lived in the vicarage in the village halfway between Exeter and Plymouth from 1630 to 1648, and from 1660 to his death, at 83, in 1674. Though at times he fought against the isolation and roughness of his provincial setting,[4] and hankered after the civilization of London, one can see the deep inspiration that the landscape of Devonshire had for Herrick in his poetry. Exiled from the capital and civilized society and culture, Herrick did have his books (his beloved *Bible* and Latin poets) as well as the friendship of his pets (they appear in his poems, sometimes in heartfelt elegies when they die – such as 'Upon His Spaniel Tracie'), his housekeeper (Prudence Baldwin), his sister, and friends at the nearby Dean Court.

Some of Robert Herrick's most delightful poems are about the wonders of nature, such as blossoms, flowers and fields ('The Shower of Blossoms', 'The Lilly in a Christal', 'To Pansies', 'To Cherry-blossomes', 'To a Bed of Tulips', 'To Laurels', 'Upon Roses', 'The Succession of Four Sweet Months', 'The Rainbow', 'To the Rose: Song', 'To Flowers', 'To Blossoms', 'To Groves', 'To Violets', 'To Carnations', 'To Sycamores', 'To Springs and Fountains', 'To Daffadills', 'To Meddowes', 'To the Willow-tree' and 'To Primroses Fill'd With Morning-dew').

For mediæval, Renaissance and Cavalier poets (like Robert Herrick). Britain would have been a much more 'pastoral' landscape than it is in the modern era. There would have many more trees, far fewer roads, no cars, planes, trains, electric lights, pylons, pipes, road signs, telephones, and so on. The landscape that poets such as Langland, Chaucer, Wyatt, Parnell, Smith, Keats and Brontë lived in was dramatically different from the urbanized world of today. There are, of course, continuities between the mediæval and Elizabethan period and now: the same rivers flow, the same birds sing (minus a few species), the same trees rustle their leaves in Autumn. It is (partly) this continuity that makes the poetry of Herrick so enduring. The relationship with nature is one of those everlasting relationships that humanity is perpetually dealing with (like the relation to the body, to God, to politics). In his poetry Herrick tackles the great themes – love, time, God, nature, the body.

Much of Robert Herrick's poetry concerns the themes and imagery of Elizabethan (and mediæval) poetry: the evocation of a pastoral, Arcadian, pre-Fall landscape, a Paradise, in fact, populated with shepherdesses, nymphs, animals and the abundance of nature. Already in the art of William Shakespeare this pastoral mythology was fading, being supplanted by a worldly knowingness (if not cynicism). Herrick's poetry, though, often harks back to a paradisal earlier age, and rues the passing of time that has changed it all (for the worse, in his opinion). We find the same Greek, Roman, Biblical, mediæval, Christian and Renaissance/ humanist themes in Herrick's work that are the staple of Elizabethan poetry.[5] As well as learned and literary, Herrick's subjects are often seemingly 'ordinary' or 'commonplace'. He writes of bucolic traditions; of old age; of bawdy times; of his mistress's breasts; of cherry blossom; of fashionable clothes (one of his famous poems is 'Delight in Disorder', where 'a careless shoestring' betokens a 'wild civility' which 'bewitches' the poet more than precision).

There are many poems in Robert Herrick's work of love – about love desired, lost and mourned. Herrick is very definitely a 'Muse poet', to use Robert Graves's term. There are many poems to several mistresses, 'my dearest Beauties' he calls them in 'To His Lovely Mistresses' (Anthea, Perilla, Electra, Blanch, Judith, Silvia, and the most beloved of all, Julia). There are many poems to certain 'muses' or 'maidens'. The sheer number (and quality) of Herrick's poems to Julia attests to his deep passion for women, the friendship and strength of women: among the 'Julia' poems are:

'To Julia', 'To Roses in Julia's Bosom', 'To the Fever Not to Trouble Julia', 'Julia's Petticoat', 'The Frozen Zone: or, Julia Disdainful', 'To Julia, in Her Dawn, or Daybreak', 'His Last Request to Julia', 'The Parliament of Roses to Julia', 'Upon Julia's Recovery', 'Upon Julia's Fall', 'His Sailing From Julia', 'His Embalming to Julia', 'Her Legs', 'Her Bed', 'On Julia's Picture', 'The Bracelet to Julia', 'A Ring Presented to Julia', 'To Julia in the Temple' and so on.

Apart from poems entitled 'To His Book', there are probably more poems in Robert Herrick's work addressed 'To Julia' than to anything else. Julia is 'the prime of *Paradise*' ('To Julia, in Her Dawn, or Day-breake'). She is utterly adored, often erotically. There are many poems which eulogize her breasts and nipples, for instance: 'Display thy breasts…/ Between whose glories, there my lips I'll lay,/ Ravisht' he writes (in 'Upon Julia's Breasts'); other pæans to Julia's breasts include 'Upon the Roses in Julia's Bosom' and 'Upon the Nipples of Julia's Breast'. Herrick makes the age-old connections between the fertility of nature outside (the rain, the lush vegetation, the rivers of the Paradisal Earth) and the bounty of women inside (Julia's breasts form a valley of abundance, as in William Shakespeare's poem 'Venus and Adonis', in which the poet would like to languish).

Women in Robert Herrick's poetry are seen as the givers of pleasure (expressed as sex), nurturance (breast milk), and all things worthy in the world (love). 'All Pleasures meet in Womankind', he writes in 'On Himself'. They are just as important in his poetry as God, the King or Christianity. Much of Herrick's poetry concerns (masculine) public, worldly, and religious themes (such as King Charles and politics, or God and the *Bible*), but just as much (more, probably) celebrates (feminine) erotic pleasure, food, nature, folk rituals, music and women, in that 'cleanly-wanton' way which is Herrick's own (the phrase, which describes much of his work, comes from the opening poem of *Hesperides*).

Robert Herrick happily fuses erotic descriptions of nature or food with lush, sensual evocations of erotic love.[6] To describe how wonderful sensual love can be, Herrick, like so many poets before him, uses the metaphor of abundant nature, expressed in flowers, trees, rivers, hills, and food. In 'To Phillis To love, and Love With Him', for example, Herrick's narrator proclaims:

> Live, live with me, and thou shalt see
> The pleasures I'll prepare for thee...

And goes into a long list of the bounty of nature: 'sweet soft Moss shall by thy bed', 'Fleeces purest Downe', 'Cream of Cowslips buttered', daisies, violets, daffodils, primroses, roses, the 'blushing Apple, bashful Peare,/ And shame-fac't Plum'. Robert Herrick's poetry is, like Percy Bysshe Shelley's or William Shakespeare's, tremendously sensual. In poem after poem he uses metaphors and images of shiny, ripe fruit, or radiant flowers, or soft grass, or silk, or fresh springwater. Images of natural abundance occur throughout his poetry. Even rain, which he would have known day after day in Dartmoor, is treated spectrally, as in 'A Conjuration to Electra', where he speaks of the 'Dewes and drisling Raine,/ That swell the Golden Graine'. Some of the most erotic poems around concerning perfume and smell are Herrick's: In 'Love Perfumes All Parts', Herrick writes of his mistress Anthea's body in a state of heightened intoxication, claiming that her hands, thighs and legs 'are all/ Richly Aromatical'. So deliciously musky is the beloved for the poet, he says she is sweeter than Juno and muskier than the Goddess Isis, no less.

Some of Robert Herrick's finest landscape poems are not about Dartmoor or Devonshire, but about London, his birthplace and beloved city. 'His Return to London' is perhaps the best of these city-poems, in which his return to the capital is seen as a yearned-for homecoming.

> O *Place! O People!* Manners! fram'd to please
> All *Nations, Customers, Kindreds, Language!*

There are poems in Robert Herrick's *œuvre* on the pleasures of music, which he calls 'thou *Queen of Heaven,* Care-charming-spell' (in 'To Musick. A Song'). The theme of the music-poems is the enchantment that music can bring. 'Charm me asleep, and melt me so/ With thy Delicious Numbers', he urges music in 'To Musique, To Becalme His Fever'. 'And make me smooth as Balme, and Oile againe', he entreats in 'To Musick'.

There are some hearty and tender pæans to holidays, feasts, festivals and rituals (pagan as well as Christian) in Robert Herrick's poetry: such as 'The Succession of Four Sweet Months', and the best of them all, 'Corinna's Going a Maying'. The celebration of the seasons and annual holidays chimes with Herrick's abiding theme of the passing of time, and the need to seize the moment and enjoy it.

It's typical of Robert Herrick, too, to mention in his nature poems the passing of time. The very first verse of his 'To

Blossoms' asks the question of the blossoms 'Why do ye fall so fast?' As soon as the beauty of the blossoms is invoked, time and death follow on immediately (echoing *sakura* as the embodiment of impermanence in Japanese culture). The line of 'To Blossoms' is 'They glide/ Into the grave.' The same protestations to nature's pleasures being over so swiftly occur in 'To Daisies, Not To Shut So Soone' and 'To Daffadills' ('we weep to see/ You haste away so soone'). In 'All Things Decay and Die' he states quite baldly: '*All things decay with Time*'.

The many poems called 'To His Book' attest to Robert Herrick's deep concern for his art – how long (or if) it will last, who will enshrine it, and soon. The same concerns with the relations between mortality, time and death and the artist and his art are central to William Shakespeare's *œuvre* (it is the guiding theme of the *Sonnets*). The key Herrickian theme is to enjoy life before death takes it away. 'While Fate permits us, let's be merry' as he puts it in 'To Enjoy the Time'. 'Every time seems so short to be' he says in 'Felicity, Quick of Flight'.

It's true that Robert Herrick did not write long poems, like John Keats or William Wordsworth (in the sense that long, 'epic' poems equal seriousness and *gravitas*),[7] but, in his own way, his nature poetry is every bit as valuable as theirs. His love-poetry is sometimes compared unfavourably with that of John Donne: again, in his own way, Herrick is every bit as fruitful a love-poet as John Donne (or Thomas Campion, Kit Marlowe, even William Shakespeare or Edmund Spenser). He was not as showy a poet as S.T. Coleridge or Alexander Pope, not so ambitious, formally, yet he is a superb writer, witty, hedonistic, impassioned, commonsensical.

# Notes

1. F.R. Leavis: *Revaluation*, Chatto & Windus 1936, 36
2. T.S. Eliot: "What is Minor Poetry?", *Swanee Review*, 54, 1946
3. Leah S. Marcus: "Robert Herrick", in Coms, 1993, 180
4. In 'Discontents in Devon' Herrick writes:

More discontents I never had
Since I was born, then here;
Where I have been, and still am sad,
In this dull *Devon-shire*...

5. In his poetry Herrick alludes to, among others, Anacreon, Horace, Catullus, Marital and other (Roman) poets, as well as Ben Jonson (whom Herrick admired) and the *Bible*.

6. As Stephen Coote puts it, in Herrick's poetry the 'sensuousness is the more telling for its sophisticated simplicity and, at its best, is returned to nature.' (Coote: *The Penguin Short History of English Literature*, Penguin 1993, 175)

7. There are lengthy poems (such as 'Upon His Kinswoman Mistress Elizabeth Herrick', 'His Age, Dedicated To His Peculiar Friend, M. John Wickes, Under the Name of Posthumus', 'A Nuptial Song, or Epithalamie, on Sir Clipseby Crew and His Lady', 'Corinna's Going a Maying', 'A Country Life: To His Brother, M. Tho: Herrick', 'The Welcome to Sack' and 'An Epithalamie to Sir Thomas Southwell and His Ladie') but nothing as long as *Prometheus Unbound* or *The Replude*.

# Bibliography

Cleanth Brooks: *The Well Wrought Urn*, Dennis Dobson 1957
A.B. Coiro: *Robert Herrick's 'Hesperides' and the Epigram Book Tradition*, John Hopkins University Press 1988
—ed: *Robert Herrick*, special no. of *George Herbert Journal* 14, 1-2, Autumn 1990
N. Coms, ed: *The Cambridge Companion to English Poetry: Donne to Marvell*, Cambridge University Press 1993
R.H. Deming: *Ceremony and Art: Robert Herrick's Poetry*, Mouton, Hague 1974
A. Leigh Deneef: *'This Poetick Liturgie': Robert Herrick's Ceremonial Mode*, Duke University Press 1974
E.H. Hageman: *Robert Herrick: A Reference Guide*, G.K. Hall, Boston 1983
G. Hammond: *Fleeting Things: English Poets and Poems 1616-1660*, Harvard University Press 1990
Robert Herrick: *The Poems of Robert Herrick*, ed. L.C. Martin, Oxford University Press 1965
—*Poems*, ed. J. Max Patrick, New York University Press 1963
—*Robert Herrick: The Hesperides and Noble Numbers*, ed. Alfred Pollard, Muse's Library, London 1891
—*The Poetical Works of Robert Herrick*, Oxford English Texts 1915
—*Hesperides: The Poems and Other Remains of Robert Herrick Now First Collected*, ed. W. Carew Hazlitt, London 1869
—*The Complete Works of Robert Herrick*, ed. Alexander B. Grosart, London 1876
—*Selected Poems*, ed. David Jesson-Dibley, Carcanet 1989
M. MacLeod: *Concordance to the Poems of Robert Herrick*, Oxford University Press, New York 1936
Leah S. Marcus: *The Politics of Mirth: Jonson, Herrick, Milton, Marvell and the Defense of Old Holiday Pastimes*, University of Chicago Press 1986

F.W. Moorman: *Robert Herrick: a Biographical and Critical Study*, Russell & Russell, New York 1910
S. Musgrove: "The Universe of Robert Herrick", *Auckland University College Bulletin*, 38, 1950
John Press: *Herrick*, Longmans, Green & Co
Roger Rollin: *Robert Herrick*, Twayne, New York 1966/92
— & J. Max Patrick, eds: *Trust to Good Verses: Herrick Tercentenary Essays*, University of Pittsburgh Press 1977
George W. Scott: *Robert Herrick,* Sidgwick & Jackson 1974

# Arseny Tarkovsky

translated and edited by Virginia Rounding

Arseny Tarkovsky is the neglected Russian poet, father of the acclaimed film director Andrei Tarkovsky. This new book gathers together many of Tarkovsky's most lyrical and heartfelt poems, in Rounding's clear, new translations. Many of Tarkovsky's poems appeared in his son's films, such as *Mirror, Stalker, Nostalghia* and *The Sacrifice*. There is an introduction by Rounding, and a bibliography of both Arseny and Andrei Tarkovsky.

Bibliography and notes  124pp  3rd ed   ISBN 9781861712660 Hbk  ISBN 9781861711144

# MAURICE SENDAK
## & the art of children's book illustration

**Maurice Sendak** is the widely acclaimed American children's book author and illustrator. This critical study focuses on his famous trilogy, *Where the Wild Things Are, In the Night Kitchen* and *Outside Over There*, as well as the early works and Sendak's superb depictions of the Grimm Brothers' fairy tales in *The Juniper Tree*. L.M. Poole begins with a chapter on children's book illustration, in particular the treatment of fairy tales. Sendak's work is situated within the history of children's book illustration, and he is compared with many contemporary authors.

Fully illustrated. The book has been revised and updated for this edition.
ISBN 9781861714282 Pbk   ISBN 9781861713469 Hbk

# Beauties, Beasts, and Enchantment

## CLASSIC FRENCH FAIRY TALES

*Translated and with an Introduction by Jack Zipes*

A collection of 36 classic French fairy tales translated by renowned writer Jack Zipes. *Cinderella*, *Beauty and the Beast*, *Sleeping Beauty* and *Little Red Riding Hood* are among the classic fairy tales in this amazing book.
Includes illustrations from fairy tale collections.
Jack Zipes has written and published widely on fairy tales.

'Terrific... a succulent array of 17th and 18th century 'salon' fairy tales'
- *The New York Times Book Review*

'These tales are adventurous, thrilling in a way fairy tales are meant to be... The translation from the French is modern, happily free of archaic and hyperbolic language... a fine and sophisticated collection' - *New York Tribune*

'Enjoyable to read... a unique collection of French regional folklore' - *Library Journal*

'Charming stories accompanied by attractive pen-and-ink drawings' - *Chattanooga Times*

Introduction and illustrations   612pp.   ISBN 9781861712510 Pbk   ISBN 9781861713193 Hbk

# CRESCENT MOON PUBLISHING

web: www.crmoon.com  e-mail: cresmopub@yahoo.co.uk

## ARTS, PAINTING, SCULPTURE

The Art of Andy Goldsworthy
Andy Goldsworthy: Touching Nature
Andy Goldsworthy in Close-Up
Andy Goldsworthy: Pocket Guide
Andy Goldsworthy In America
Land Art: A Complete Guide
The Art of Richard Long
Richard Long: Pocket Guide
Land Art In the UK
Land Art in Close-Up
Land Art In the U.S.A.
Land Art: Pocket Guide
Installation Art in Close-Up
Minimal Art and Artists In the 1960s and After
Colourfield Painting
Land Art DVD, TV documentary
Andy Goldsworthy DVD, TV documentary
The Erotic Object: Sexuality in Sculpture From Prehistory to the Present Day
Sex in Art: Pornography and Pleasure in Painting and Sculpture
Postwar Art
Sacred Gardens: The Garden in Myth, Religion and Art
Glorification: Religious Abstraction in Renaissance and 20th Century Art
Early Netherlandish Painting
Leonardo da Vinci
Piero della Francesca
Giovanni Bellini
Fra Angelico: Art and Religion in the Renaissance
Mark Rothko: The Art of Transcendence
Frank Stella: American Abstract Artist
Jasper Johns
Brice Marden
Alison Wilding: The Embrace of Sculpture
Vincent van Gogh: Visionary Landscapes
Eric Gill: Nuptials of God
Constantin Brancusi: Sculpting the Essence of Things
Max Beckmann
Caravaggio
Gustave Moreau
Egon Schiele: Sex and Death In Purple Stockings
Delizioso Fotografico Fervore: Works In Process 1
Sacro Cuore: Works In Process 2
The Light Eternal: J.M.W. Turner
The Madonna Glorified: Karen Arthurs

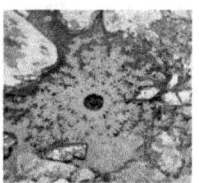

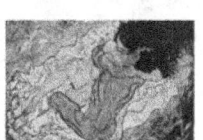

# LITERATURE

J.R.R. Tolkien: The Books, The Films, The Whole Cultural Phenomenon
J.R.R. Tolkien: Pocket Guide
Tolkien's Heroic Quest
The *Earthsea* Books of Ursula Le Guin
Beauties, Beasts and Enchantment: Classic French Fairy Tales
German Popular Stories by the Brothers Grimm
Philip Pullman and *His Dark Materials*
Sexing Hardy: Thomas Hardy and Feminism
Thomas Hardy's *Tess of the d'Urbervilles*
Thomas Hardy's *Jude the Obscure*
Thomas Hardy: The Tragic Novels
Love and Tragedy: Thomas Hardy
The Poetry of Landscape in Hardy
Wessex Revisited: Thomas Hardy and John Cowper Powys
Wolfgang Iser: Essays and Interviews
Petrarch, Dante and the Troubadours
Maurice Sendak and the Art of Children's Book Illustration
Andrea Dworkin

Cixous, Irigaray, Kristeva: The *Jouissance* of French Feminism
Julia Kristeva: Art, Love, Melancholy, Philosophy, Semiotics and Psychoanalysis
Hélene Cixous I Love You: The *Jouissance* of Writing
Luce Irigaray: Lips, Kissing, and the Politics of Sexual Difference
Peter Redgrove: Here Comes the Flood
Peter Redgrove: Sex-Magic-Poetry-Cornwall
Lawrence Durrell: Between Love and Death, East and West
Love, Culture & Poetry: Lawrence Durrell
Cavafy: Anatomy of a Soul
German Romantic Poetry: Goethe, Novalis, Heine, Hölderlin
Feminism and Shakespeare
Shakespeare: Love, Poetry & Magic
The Passion of D.H. Lawrence
D.H. Lawrence: Symbolic Landscapes
D.H. Lawrence: Infinite Sensual Violence
Rimbaud: Arthur Rimbaud and the Magic of Poetry
The Ecstasies of John Cowper Powys
Sensualism and Mythology: The Wessex Novels of John Cowper Powys
Amorous Life: John Cowper Powys and the Manifestation of Affectivity (H.W. Fawkner)
Postmodern Powys: New Essays on John Cowper Powys (Joe Boulter)
Rethinking Powys: Critical Essays on John Cowper Powys
Paul Bowles & Bernardo Bertolucci
Rainer Maria Rilke

Joseph Conrad: *Heart of Darkness*
In the Dim Void: Samuel Beckett
Samuel Beckett Goes into the Silence
André Gide: Fiction and Fervour
Jackie Collins and the Blockbuster Novel
Blinded By Her Light: The Love-Poetry of Robert Graves
The Passion of Colours: Travels In Mediterranean Lands
Poetic Forms

## POETRY

Ursula Le Guin: Walking In Cornwall
Peter Redgrove: Here Comes The Flood
Peter Redgrove: Sex-Magic-Poetry-Cornwall
Dante: Selections From the Vita Nuova
Petrarch, Dante and the Troubadours
William Shakespeare: Sonnets
William Shakespeare: Complete Poems
Blinded By Her Light: The Love-Poetry of Robert Graves
Emily Dickinson: Selected Poems
Emily Brontë: Poems
Thomas Hardy: Selected Poems
Percy Bysshe Shelley: Poems
John Keats: Selected Poems
Joh n Keats: Poems of 1820
D.H. Lawrence: Selected Poems
Edmund Spenser: Poems
Edmund Spenser: Amoretti
John Donne: Poems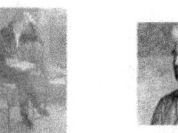
Henry Vaughan: Poems
Sir Thomas Wyatt: Poems
Robert Herrick: Selected Poems
Rilke: Space, Essence and Angels in the Poetry of Rainer Maria Rilke
Rainer Maria Rilke: Selected Poems
Friedrich Hölderlin: Selected Poems
Arseny Tarkovsky: Selected Poems
Arthur Rimbaud: Selected Poems
Arthur Rimbaud: A Season in Hell
Arthur Rimbaud and the Magic of Poetry
Novalis: Hymns To the Night
German Romantic Poetry
Paul Verlaine: Selected Poems
Elizaethan Sonnet Cycles
D.J. Enright: By-Blows
Jeremy Reed: Brigitte's Blue Heart
Jeremy Reed: Claudia Schiffer's Red Shoes
Gorgeous Little Orpheus
Radiance: New Poems
Crescent Moon Book of Nature Poetry
Crescent Moon Book of Love Poetry
Crescent Moon Book of Mystical Poetry
Crescent Moon Book of Elizabethan Love Poetry
Crescent Moon Book of Metaphysical Poetry
Crescent Moon Book of Romantic Poetry
Pagan America: New American Poetry

## MEDIA, CINEMA, FEMINISM and CULTURAL STUDIES

J.R.R. Tolkien: The Books, The Films, The Whole Cultural Phenomenon
J.R.R. Tolkien: Pocket Guide
The *Lord of the Rings* Movies: Pocket Guide
The Cinema of Hayao Miyazaki
Hayao Miyazaki: *Princess Mononoke*: Pocket Movie Guide
Hayao Miyazaki: *Spirited Away*: Pocket Movie Guide
Tim Burton : Hallowe'en For Hollywood
Ken Russell
Ken Russell: *Tommy*: Pocket Movie Guide
The Ghost Dance: The Origins of Religion
The Peyote Cult

Cixous, Irigaray, Kristeva: The *Jouissance* of French Feminism
Julia Kristeva: Art, Love, Melancholy, Philosophy, Semiotics and Psychoanalysis
Luce Irigaray: Lips, Kissing, and the Politics of Sexual Difference
Hélene Cixous I Love You: The *Jouissance* of Writing
Andrea Dworkin
'Cosmo Woman': The World of Women's Magazines
Women in Pop Music
HomeGround: The Kate Bush Anthology
Discovering the Goddess (Geoffrey Ashe)
The Poetry of Cinema
The Sacred Cinema of Andrei Tarkovsky
Andrei Tarkovsky: Pocket Guide
Andrei Tarkovsky: *Mirror*: Pocket Movie Guide
Andrei Tarkovsky: *The Sacrifice*: Pocket Movie Guide
Walerian Borowczyk: Cinema of Erotic Dreams
Jean-Luc Godard: The Passion of Cinema
Jean-Luc Godard: *Hail Mary*: Pocket Movie Guide
Jean-Luc Godard: *Contempt*: Pocket Movie Guide
Jean-Luc Godard: *Pierrot le Fou*: Pocket Movie Guide
John Hughes and Eighties Cinema
*Ferris Bueller's Day Off*: Pocket Movie Guide
Jean-Luc Godard: Pocket Guide
The Cinema of Richard Linklater
Liv Tyler: Star In Ascendance
*Blade Runner* and the Films of Philip K. Dick
Paul Bowles and Bernardo Bertolucci
Media Hell: Radio, TV and the Press
An Open Letter to the BBC
Detonation Britain: Nuclear War in the UK
Feminism and Shakespeare
Wild Zones: Pornography, Art and Feminism
Sex in Art: Pornography and Pleasure in Painting and Sculpture
Sexing Hardy: Thomas Hardy and Feminism

*The Light Eternal* is a model monograph, an exemplary job. The subject matter of the book is beautifully organised and dead on beam. (Lawrence Durrell)

It is amazing for me to see my work treated with such passion and respect. (Andrea Dworkin)

### CRESCENT MOON PUBLISHING
P.O. Box 1312, Maidstone, Kent, ME14 5XU, Great Britain. www.crmoon.com

cresmopub@yahoo.co.uk   www.crescentmoon.org.uk